SEIZING : PLACES

Hélène Dorion

SEIZING : PLACES

RAVIR : LES LIEUX

Translated and introduced by
Patrick McGuinness

2012

Published by Arc Publications
Nanholme Mill, Shaw Wood Road
Todmorden OL14 6DA, UK
www.arcpublications.co.uk

Copyright in the poems © Editions de la Différence 2005
Translation copyright © Patrick McGuinness 2012
Introduction copyright © Patrick McGuinness 2012
Copyright in the present edition © Arc Publications 2012

Design by Tony Ward
Printed in Great Britain by the MPG Book Group,
Bodmin and King's L ynn

978 1906570 12 5 (pbk)
978 1906570 17 0 (hbk)

Hélène Dorion's poems in the original French
are reproduced by kind permission of
Éditions de la Différence
www.ladifference.fr

Cover image by Uzia Ograbek

Supported using public funding by
ARTS COUNCIL
ENGLAND
LOTTERY FUNDED

'Arc Translations' Series Editor: Jean Boase-Beier

CONTENTS

Introduction / 7

Hélène Dorion was born in 1958 in Quebec City, and now lives in Montreal. She studied philosophy at Laval University (Quebec), and published her first collection of poems, *L'Intervalle prolongé*, in 1983. Since then her prolific *œuvre* – poetry, fiction, essays, and *livres d'artistes* – has constituted one of modern Quebecois literature's major achievements. She is the winner of the Governor General's Award for Poetry, the Prix Mallarmé, the Prix Wallonie-Bruxelles, the Prix Alain-Grandbois, and numerous other Canadian and international prizes. When *Ravir: les lieux* appeared in 2005, Dorion became the first Canadian to receive the Prix Mallarmé, while her 2008 collection of poems, *Le Hublot des heures*, won the Prix Charles-Vildrac – another first for a Quebecois writer. In 2011, Dorion won the European Prix Léopold-Senghor.

Dorion has accomplished a great deal in a relatively short time, not just as a writer but as an editor: she was editor for one of the major poetry publishing houses in Quebec, Le Noroît, between 1991 and 2000, sits on the boards of various literary magazines and prize juries, and has produced important critical work on Quebecois and French-language poetry, including an edition of the modernist Quebecois poet, Saint-Denis Garneau. In 2002, the poet and critic Pierre Nepveu published a selection of her poetry, entitled *D'Argile et de souffle*, and in 2006 a collected poems appeared from Editions de l'Hexagone entitled *Mondes fragiles, choses frêles*.

Though Dorion's poetry has evolved, it has always been limpid and intense, sophisticated in its thinking but elemental in its feel for the world. It is also emphatic about poetry's role in knowing that world, in putting the world to words not in order to name it, pin it down and categorise it, but because expressing the world is also to experience it. As she writes in her essay "Living in Poetry", 'Poetry is as much a state of being as a mode of writing', and in the same text she describes poetry as a means of 'crossing' language. It is a verb that tells us a great deal about Dorion's approach. Some poets think of themselves as 'using' language, others of being 'used by' it, and all poets rely on particular verbs, particular metaphors, to figure their relationship with language. In Dorion's case, to *cross* language implies a trajectory through it, an immersion in it, but also the possibility of language as obstacle as well as destination. Throughout her poetic *œuvre* we find a probing, tentative consciousness, as comfortable with the idioms of philosophy as with the language of lyric poetry. It is the way the two work together, keeping each other's excesses in check – thought enriched by feeling, feeling kept in perspective by thought – that characterises her most penetrating work. This is not poetry that launches itself at its subject, but that feels its way around it. Intensity of expression and attentiveness of vision combine to render a sense of the world distilled, and of a language at its most expansive when it is most stripped down and resistant to rhetorical transports.

Ravir: les lieux, translated here as *Seizing: Places*, is perhaps her most ambitious work so far, and though Dorion has written plenty since its publication, there is something culminative about this book. It is subtitled "Poèmes", a plural that refuses totality though not coherence, and is made of five sequences: 'Ravir: les villes', 'Ravir: les ombres', 'Ravir: les miroirs', 'Ravir: les fenêtres', and 'Ravir: les visages': cities, shadows, mirrors, windows and faces… The verb *ravir* has so many shades of meaning – to ravish, seize, entrance, plunder, abduct… – that it seems impossible to find a single English verb that would do all the original's ambiguous – and ambiguating – work. It is related to our word *rapture*, and posits, too, the poet as *raptor*, as well as the one *rapt* and *enraptured* by the world. In addition to the problems such a multi-faceted word as

8

ravir causes the translator, it is worth signalling the ways in which it works across its many connotations in this book. First, and perhaps most obviously, the poet is enraptured, ravished, captivated by the world. But her task is to capture it in language, to seize it the way one might 'seize' an essence or an image. But language too has its lure, is all too easy to be captivated by. These poetic seizings or ravishings are not merely descriptive or mimetic; they are distillations, intensities of perception, memory, reflection and experience that themselves take hold of language, plunder it, leave it exhausted. This is something Dorion's poetry does well: though the language is often tentative and probing, it is always ready to rise to the high style; she will use abstractions and is not afraid of words like 'soul' and 'void', words which, to the anglophone ear, might seem to mean so much that they threaten to end up meaning not enough.

The world enraptures us, but we in turn use it, and use it up. Indeed, the way language plunders the world and the way we plunder the world's resources are part of a subtly framed correlation in Dorion's poetry, and one of its most daring propositions: we seek meanings from it, prospecting for symbols and digging for significance from landscapes or skies or urban scenes the way one digs for water or prospects for oil.

There is little by way of visual description in Dorion's poetry, and yet it is full of moments of intense visuality: verbs of seeing and perception abound, while the senses generally – touch, taste, hearing, sight – play a large role in this poetry, which remains close to the senses even at its most cerebral and abstract. It is an unusual combination, but it accounts for the sense Dorion gives us at once of poetry's slender hold upon the real, and of the massy, weighty pull of language, along with language's own distortions and opacities. The lines, with their variable lengths, refuse the tidiness of endstops and are light on punctuation. They are often short and rhythmic, built less around grammatical units than a sort of tempo of perception: the pauses are weighted, the words hang for a moment on the edge of the line, feeling the obstacle and testing the drop, then dip into the next line, the next verset. The page's native blankness surrounds the lines but also ventilates them, so that the poems occupy their pages with a precarious centrality. That centrality is also modest and unpresumptuous: the poems are crossed with blankness, just as, we imagine, the poet's thoughts are crossed with the chaos and the darkness that would abolish them. Their solidity on the page seems always on the verge of dissolving at the edges, and the poem too invokes edges as places of revelation and plenitude, but also of risk: between earth and sky, between water and land, but also between word and word, language and silence, the written page and the blank page. 'Writing does not protect me from life's turbulence, but rather takes me to its most precarious points of equilibrium, where the sense of provisionality is at its sharpest', she writes in her essay, "The Poem's Detail".

There is in Dorion a constant feeling for the chaos, the non-meaning, the void, impinging on the slender edifices of sense we that we create. The poet creates her edifices with words, but others create them with figures or formulae, with compasses, graphs, musical notes, paint and canvas, bricks and mortar, tools or machines. One of the convictions in *Ravir: les lieux* is that poetry, and literature more generally, is another of the ways by which we make sense of the world. If there seems to be an existential tenor to all this, that is because there is: for Dorion, poetry is a means of orientation in existence, a way of being as well as a way of knowing. This poetry has accepted a dose of darkness, a fleck of the abyss, as a sort of vaccine; hence that sense we have of Dorion's clarities being surrounded at times by a sort of teeming threat of chaos or oblivion. But though Dorion is not – and certainly not, by Quebecois standards – an overtly political poet, she is a poet quite clearly engaged in the social and political realities of the world outside. The elemental nature of her poetry does not prevent it from being topical or urgent in ways that translate directly into contemporary issues. This is not poetry in retreat, but rather a poetry that presents an alternative to what she memorably calls, in her essay "The Open Window", 'the chessboard where the only movements allowed are ruled by the verbs *to have*, *to produce*, and *to seem*'.

To read Dorion's poetry is to feel the words themselves thickening, gaining dimension, becoming equal to their task. But they are simple words, most of the time – what makes them difficult or complex is their nakedness and their compression. There is no excess either, nothing is overdescribed, no line overladen, and the poems' moments of greatest emotional effect are when one mode reaches a kind of tipping point; when, for instance, a series of visual or sense perceptions peak in intensity, seem to crowd in, then suddenly *segue* into something expansive and almost spiritual in its clarity. However intense and physical the experience, its vanishing point is always a spiritual one – the two are, in Dorion, part of a continuum, perhaps indeed translations of each other. This is one of Dorion's trademarks: the world comes in from our eyes, touch, smell, the inchoate mass of wordless feelings, sensations, those tropistic alterations by which we change internally, unnoticed even by ourselves. Then language makes room for it, is rendered dynamic by the necessity of rendering these experiences in a way that can be understood, and not in some contorted private idiom. One of the ways in which that sense of urgency is carried is found in Dorion's use of the word *tu*: it interpolates the reader, makes us protagonists of what is unfolding, fellow-travellers in the poem's motion. We too are 'crossing' language.

Dorion is adept at the sequence, and her poetry has always had a probing, self-refashioning and self-revisiting tendency that works well in the sequence form. In *Ravir: les lieux* we have the slow-burning, cumulative mode of a book that gives itself the time and space to unfold, but that allows itself the page-by-page intensities of the fragmentary. Indeed Dorion's is not so much fragmentary thinking as thinking-by-fragments, a very different proposition, because it binds together the very brokenness it proceeds by, and creates a sort of mosaicised mode of poetry. In the first poem of *Ravir: les lieux* she describes the 'impossible / silent mosaic of the journey', and that nicely catches both the questing nature of her poetry, the journey of and in language, and her poems' ability to bring the broken edges into alignment and create patterns from the individual pieces. This is what gives her work its sense of hesitancy and danger, of being on the edge of dissolution, and at the same time driven by a consciousness that threads its perceptions together, that transforms vision into insight. We see this for instance in her use of verbs of binding and cohesion on the one hand and of dissolution and scattering on the other.

Despite the elemental nature of her poetry, there is a weight of literature there, a cultural freight that plays an important role in framing the poems and in evincing an idea of the poet's vocation. Dorion does not pretend that she is making the world anew or seeing it for the first time. There are no false unities, idealised returns or mythical origins. This is one of the book's characteristic achievements: there is no artificial barrier between the made world – the world of poetry, art, fiction, and the cultural markers that Dorion sparingly uses – and the found world of lakes and mountains and oceans that we all too easily place under the rubric 'ecology'. The poem is as much 'at home' (a phrase Dorion would enjoy the irony of...) in the city, in a library, on a busy highway, as it is under the expansive open skies of the prairie. Dorion's poetry makes a nonsense of the false opposition between so-called nature and so-called artifice: we live among what we make as much as what we find. The parking meter measures our time as well as the solar cycle...

We should also remember that Quebecois literature, for all its French heritage, is also a North American literature, and that this seeming juxtaposition of the inherited culture and the found land accounts for the exhilarating strangeness of Quebecois poetry, its alertness to the paradoxes of place, the lures of belonging. Dorion may be a cosmopolitan and international poet, but her poetry is rooted in its landscape too: the wide open spaces, the lakes and mountains, the big skies, the seasons and weather of Quebec; she is also attuned to its urbanism, its cultural accretions, its unique paradox of newness and age.

There are big themes in this book: history playing its 'greatest hits', the 'century's boneyard', the collision of personal biography with collective experience, the knowledge of place as habitat (cities, streets, buildings) alongside more abstract spiritual orientation in space. There are archetypes too, mythic but also contemporary in their relevance: the Geographer, the Navigator, the Carpenter... along with writers such as Woolf and Rilke and Guidacci, and the mathematician Hypatia. The cities of Dorion's imagination are Berlin, London, Paris, Montreal, but she also describes the spiritual power of landscape, and our hankering for its absent meanings. Dorion's poetry bridges modes of knowledge, and we might say too that its scale is epic, though there is nothing Olympian or sweeping about her way of knowing the world. On the contrary, it is probing, ear-to-the-ground, eye-to-the-surface poetry; it

13

trusts to the senses, to the vagaries of thought, is ready to take up and let go of motifs in a way that remains organic and changeable.

To the ear attuned to the modalities of English-language poetry, this way of writing will probably be unfamiliar. After all, we in English-language poetry write as if we somehow disdained poetry but had faith in language – it's a facet of our national irony perhaps, our suspicion of abstraction, and a sense that poetry somehow denatures ordinary speech. Our quest for the demotic and the democratic makes us suspicious of the grand claims of poetry, and of its grand words: the soul, memory, the spirit, and the quasi-philosophical, spiritual language by which much European and some North American poetry has orientated itself. French-language poetry, one might say, is the other way around: it suspects language, which is why French poets always seem to be remaking it, asking the impossible of it, making it fail on a scale which makes mere success look petty. But it retains its faith in poetry: the lyric urge, however broken its movement, damaged its materials, or ironic its gestures, retains its necessity. For Paul Valéry, poetry was not just a language within a language, but an operation performed on language. Poetry may reclaim its birthright from music, Valéry contended, but it always repays it debt to thought. Dorion's work is in this tradition.

Patrick McGuinness

I

SEIZING : CITIES
RAVIR : LES VILLES

¶

D'ici bouge la lumière. Regarde
le vide lourd sur l'épaule
éparpillé parmi les fenêtres.

Cherche ce que tu appelles, l'impossible
mosaïque silencieuse du voyage
et la lampe qu'on dirait brûlée
par le temps. Regarde seulement la pièce
où résonne ta vie. L'ombre jamais vue
visible maintenant, dans les yeux du soir.

¶

Entre toutes terres, le centre, la maison
plus au centre, le jardin: sillons
que tu racles, bêche de l'âme
tirant vers toi le soleil
les eaux de pluies sur les pétales
à peine apparus. Au cœur de ce monde
la chair noircie du nom, théâtre des choses
que tu livres aux vents. Quel oiseau naît
de l'oiseau blessé? Tu refais ta demeure
chaque jour, on imagine le sol
sous la main, l'arbre haut des saisons
le ciel planté dans la fenêtre, le geste superbe.

16

¶

Here is where the light moves from. Look
at the emptiness heavy on your shoulder
scattered among the windows.

Seek what you call out for, the impossible
silent mosaic of the journey
and the lamp that seems burned out
by time. Look only at the room
where your life echoes. The shadow never seen
visible now, in the night's eyes.

¶

Among all the territories, the centre, the house
and closer to the centre, the garden: furrows
that you scrape, the soul's spade
pulling the sun towards you
rainwater onto the fresh
petals. At the heart of this world
the name's blackened flesh, theatre of all
you cast to the winds. What bird is born
of the wounded bird? You rebuild your dwelling
each day, imagine the ground
beneath your hand, the seasons' topmost tree
the sky rooted in the window, its gesture sublime.

¶

Un peu partout, des images
des villes. Mers et montagnes
et maisons s'entassent
mais un seul voyage
ainsi s'effeuille.

Des papiers s'affolent, dévorent la nuit.
Grandiront dans ta bouche.
On allume des flammes, de minuscules pierres
que l'on disperse autour de toi

et bientôt tu confonds les ombres
avec les signes vivants de ton corps.

¶

Ici l'escalier d'où monte
et redescend l'histoire, en ce détail
que tu incarnes. Des mots poussés
derrière le silence. Peu importe
l'espace qui te laisse à toi-même

– et flotte entre ces murs, le craquement des objets –
tu vois la fenêtre, là remue le monde
un vent d'aube, et les notes du piano
lentement tournoient.

¶

Scattered around, images
towns. Seas and mountains
and houses pile up
but it's only one journey
being stripped bare.

A panic of papers, devouring the night.
They will grow in your mouth.
Flames are lit, tiny stones
dispersed around you

and soon you confuse your shadows
with your body's signs of life.

¶

Here, the staircase that
history climbs and climbs back down, in the single
detail you make flesh. Words pushed
behind the silence. No matter
the space that leaves you to yourself

– and floats between these walls, the scraping of objects –
you see the window, that's where the world stirs
a dawn wind, and the notes of a piano
spiralling slowly.

Tu poses le pied, c'est la mer
qui te dénoue. Tu oublies presque la plaie
la pierre gisante, sur le fil de la mémoire.
Depuis des années, tu regardes les branches
comme des racines, qui s'approchent enfin.

¶

Écoute, comme une ombre
s'avancerait, la mer, l'inlassable
vol des vagues qui claquent
contre la terre, écoute

ce monde devenu monde, à force
de résonner parmi les ans. Ton enfance
est cette matière fossile, un vœu
du temps qui brûle à mesure.

Écoute, et l'oiseau fuira encore
brisant tes châteaux sur le sable

de cette côte de l'Atlantique
où tu vis s'en aller l'aube
et revenir par tant de marées.

You put down your foot, it's the sea
unbinding you. You almost forget the wound
the dying stone, on memory's thread.
For years you have watched the branches
like roots; they are closing on you at last.

¶

Listen, the way a shadow
might advance, the sea, the unceasing
flight of the waves clattering
against the earth, listen

to this world that has become a world by force
of echoing through the years. Your childhood
is this fossil-matter, time's
desire burning as it grows.

Listen, and the bird will flee again
leaving your castles ruined along the sands

of this Atlantic coast
where you watched the sunset dissipate
and then return across so many tides.

21

¶

Tout autour t'encercle
la saison, pareille aux ossements du ciel
à cette moelle froide des jours

que poussent à mesure les nuages.
(Gorge
qui referme l'horizon
bouche de feuillage jailli, le corps léger
comme un oiseau, se blottit).

Bientôt le vent
l'eau s'échouent à tes pieds
– s'arrête le paysage.

¶

Ici l'espace de la chambre
rétrécit, à force de battre
le cœur et le temps
se livrent au monde.
Tu reconnais

ce goût de sable sur la langue
la douleur que fait la mort
parmi des couloirs immaculés.

¶

All around you the season
circles, like the sky's bones
like the days' cold marrow

growing cloud by cloud.
(Throat
closing on the horizon
a mouth of flown leaves, the body, light
as a bird, crouches).

Soon the wind
the water crash at your feet
– the landscape stops.

¶

Here the limits of your room
shrink, as they beat
heart and time
give themselves up to the world.
You recognise

that taste of sand on the tongue
the pain death spreads
along the immaculate corridors.

Tu ramènes jusqu'à ta chambre
un plein silence. Tu comptes les fleurs
sur les murs, regardes l'ombre
encore inaccomplie, et le temps
se retourne à mesure.

¶

Le lac: on dirait parfois
le désert, parfois la mer.
L'ovale certain
d'une Terre, un monde clos
avec des histoires qui tournent
au-dedans. Des fils, des nœuds
– lopins de mots dans la maison –
empêchent d'entendre

l'eau qui fuit.
Mais regarde encore:
le ciel mince
touche la tête
ravit les lieux.

¶

Le flot des cloches avait cessé
les oiseaux s'étaient tus, le chemin

You bring a full silence
back to your room. You count the flowers
on the walls, watch the shadow
still unformed, and then time
turns over.

¶

The lake: sometimes
it seems a desert, sometimes the sea.
The perfect oval
of Earth, a closed world
with stories turning
inside it. Threads, knots
– patches of words inside the house –
stop our ears against

the flowing water.
But look again:
the narrow sky
touches your head
seizes the place.

¶

The cascade of bells had stopped
the birds were quiet, the path

se perdait à mesure. Au-dessus de la ville
le ciel promenait ses gris.
Dans les arbres, il ne restait
que les os maigres du souvenir.

J'étais ici. Mais où
suis-je donc
maintenant que reviennent les forêts
les rivages et les déserts où s'obstine la braise?
Les mots reprennent leur cours, je ne suis
nulle part, en même temps
je tourne comme jadis
tournaient les oiseaux, et une fois
pour toujours.

¶

Le vent appuie sur le navire –
la mer contemple l'île –
avec leurs traînées de salive sur les lèvres
les vagues avancent, résonnent
comme des syllabes contre la coque
la lumière s'abat
jusqu'à la nuit, enserre le navire.

Dans le vide, le vent creuse
de lourdes racines que recueillent les voiles
aussitôt rabattues sur les épines.

was disappearing as it went. Above the town
the sky walked its greys.
In the trees, only
the scrawny bones of memory remained.

I was here. But where
am I
now that the rivers are returning
the forests, the deserts where the embers still burn?
words find their path again, I am
nowhere, at the same time
I turn as once
the birds turned, once
and for ever.

¶

The wind presses the boat –
the sea contemplates the island –
the waves, furrows of saliva on their lips
advance, resonate
like syllables against the hull
the light beats down
until nightfall, tightens around the boat.

In the emptiness, the wind digs
heavy roots that the sails
gather as they fall back against the thorns.

Bientôt tout un jardin
de présences s'écoule
– que tu ne cesses d'entendre.

¶

Chaque chose – tu la mâches
l'avales, secoues la tête –
chaque chose fixe en elle
des traînées de rêves
qui s'effilochent sur les murs
des ans, fondent, une fois rendues
au bout de leur ombre.

Mais le monde, – regarde
le monde s'infiltre par ta fenêtre
et l'arbre
et la branche et le bourgeon passent
en chaque chose
vois la figure des siècles
qui se bousculent dans le ciel léger
l'innombrable jardin de ta vie.

¶

Au bout des chemins, la maison. Des arbres
l'enserrent, – l'onde fragile du temps.
Le remous, plein la fenêtre.

Soon a whole garden
of presences flows
– you never stop hearing it.

¶

Each thing – you chew it over
swallow it, shake your head –
each thing fixes in itself
a foliage of dreams
dappling the walls
of the years, melting, reaching the tips
of their shadows.

But the world, – look
the world eases in through your window
and the tree
and the branch and the bud pass through
each thing
see the outline of the centuries
as they jostle in the weightless sky
the innumerable garden of your life.

¶

At the end of the paths, the house. Enclosed
by trees, – the fragile wave of time.
Movement, filling the window.

29

Tout ce qui est advenu brûle encore
livré aux nuages qui sillonnent l'horizon
et s'amoncellent comme des semences.
Lampe, table, chaise. Une vie
où chaque ici repose
sur la branche du souvenir
qui ne se rompt.

¶

Désormais le lac – le froid
le rétrécit – ouvre la fente
par où surgit la saison.

L'œuf brisé se répand
le long des rives
tandis qu'au centre, pareille pulsation
des eaux enchâsse le naufragé.

Ta vie se recroqueville
comme une bête
tu lèches la plaie.

¶

Loin du grondement, loin
de la nuit qui s'entrouvre
et nous assourdit, quels crocs

All that has happened still burns
open to the clouds that edge the horizon
scattered like seeds.
Lamp, table, chair. A life
where each *here* rests
on memory's un-
breaking branch.

¶

Henceforth the lake – the cold
shrinks it – pries open the crack
through which the season bursts.

The shattered egg spreads
along the banks
while at the centre, the same pulsation
of water encloses the shipwrecked.

Your life shrinks back
like an animal
you lick the wound.

¶

Far from the growling, far
from the gaping, deafening
night, what hooks

raclent et rongent
ton cœur, – quel ciel se renverse
sur l'histoire où tu revois la place
la fontaine Saint-Michel? Et tes pas soudain
s'engouffrent au milieu de l'obscurité.

Voilà donc ce que nous possédons
d'une ville: l'ombre qu'elle fait
dans nos corps, le battement
au loin, le battement
proche de sa langue.

¶

Forclose la ville, désassemblée
évide l'espace du passé.

La lune, l'eau, le va-et-vient
des berges, – vaine traversée
où se brise l'île incise.

Par tant de façades, tu disperses la pierre
rivée à l'histoire par tant de rues
tu cherches l'onde nouée.
L'arête et le désir. Vertige comme tu vas
vers cette spirale que n'épuisent nos bouches.

scratch and tear
your heart, – what sky overturns
itself on history where once again you see the square
the Saint-Michel fountain? And your footsteps
are suddenly buried in the darkness.

So that's what we possess
of a city: the shadow it makes
in our bodies, the far-off beat
the nearby beat
of its language.

¶

The city shut down, disassembled
hollows out the past's space.

The moon, the water, the lapping
of the banks, – vain crossing
where the cleft island breaks.

By so many façades, you disperse the stone
riveted to history by so many streets
you seek the knotted wave.
The ridge and the desire. Vertigo as you move
towards this spiral our mouths never reach the end of.

¶

Tu n'entends jamais la même musique
parmi la foule qui avance
avec toi, comme un derviche
sur la place de la Bastille, rue Mahler
dans le Marais, ta vie
tourne aussi. Des visages

suivent le tracé des ans
depuis la place d'Italie
jusqu'à Montmartre, – lampadaires
fontaines et tours s'accordent au paysage
que brûle le temps.

Sur la carte, ton doigt migrateur
écarte la poussière, des histoires
– saltimbanques, fabriquants d'étoiles –
se referment comme des volets.

¶

Après l'averse, la lumière sur les toits
inégaux redescend, lambeaux de ville
alors que le Peintre arpente le quai
Alexandre, d'une rive à l'autre, rêve:
des cerfs-volants dévorent le ciel
et promènent dans leur bec
ces haillons de silence.

¶

You never hear the same music that you hear
in the crowd that pushes forward
with you, like a dervish
on Place de la Bastille, rue Mahler
in the Marais, your life
turns too. Faces

follow the thread of the years
from Place d'Italie
to Montmartre, – streetlamps
fountains and towers in step with the landscape
burned by time.

On the map, your migrant finger
brushes off the dust, the stories
– acrobats, star-makers –
come down like shutters.

¶

After the downpour, the light climbs down
the haphazard roofs, the city in patches
as the Painter climbs the quai
Alexandre, from one bank to the other, dreaming:
kites devour the sky
ribbons of silence in their beaks.

Un siècle essaimé – l'image s'achève –
parmi les aboiements, les klaxons
entends le grondement des rames, vois
la cité s'éveille.

A century dispersed – the image takes shape –
in the barking carhorns
hear the scraping of oars, see
the city is waking.

II

Seizing : Shadows
Ravir : les ombres

¶

Tu traverses l'ombre de la ville
le paysage défait des heures
et c'est l'ombre de tes pas, l'histoire
en toi qu'elle révèle, – mondes flous
troués de matière et vertige
quand tu lèves les bras, l'insecte
plane au-dessus du puits.

À l'entrée, on mendie quelques miettes.
Le visible cède sous son poids.

Il n'est de voyage
qu'en cette forme heurtée
du regard, cette boussole qui te déplace.
Et la route se dérobe, révèle
d'autres mondes, d'autres voyages.
Tu deviens pour toi-même
désert et limite, la frontière éclatée.

Il reste des taches de vies
au bord des jours, ces visages
que l'ombre a cessé d'enfouir.

¶

Le temps avance sur ses propres traces
qu'il ne reconnaît pas. Un vieillard

¶

You cross the shadow of the town
the loose landscape of the hours
and it's the shadow of your steps, history
revealing itself in you, – blurred worlds
holed with matter, vertigo
when you raise your arms, the insect
hovering above the well.

At the entrance, someone begs a few crumbs.
The visible gives way beneath its weight.

All the journey is in
this flickering movement of the eye
the compass pushing you from place to place.
And the road disappears, reveals
other worlds, other journeys.
You become desert
to yourself, a limit, a burst frontier.

Only a few marks of other lives
are left on the edge of the days, those faces
the darkness has stopped burying.

¶

Time follows its own tracks
without recognising them. An old man

traverse la place qu'il croit déserte.
Le présent court derrière sa mémoire.

«Maintenant on fait la file
pour Rien. On n'emporte rien de soi
de l'autre côté des murs. Tout
désormais sera compté.»

Un enfant sur une balançoire
construit des rêves, la tête pleine
de mondes qu'il verra s'effondrer.

¶

Les fenêtres crachent. La vie
par la fenêtre. *Qui sommes-nous?*
D'où venons-nous?
Quelle histoire fait de l'ombre

au-dessus de nous? Des bouches anonymes
sécrètent des gouttes d'encre pâle.
Dans la tête, tout
devient plus grand:
maisons, villes, avions.
Triomphes et tragédies.

On n'a rien vu venir, et tout
soudain arrive. Derrière ce qui s'effondre
reste des ombres, que des ombres.

crosses the square he thinks is empty.
The present catches up with what he remembers.

'People queue
for Nothing these days. You can't take anything
with you beyond these walls. From
now on everything will be counted.'

A child on a swing
builds dreams, his head full
of worlds he will see collapsing.

¶

The windows spit. Life
through the window. *Who are we?*
Where do we come from?
What history casts that shadow

over us? Anonymous mouths
rolling droplets of pale ink.
In our head, everything
grows bigger:
houses, towns, aeroplanes.
Triumphs and tragedies.

We never saw it coming, and now
suddenly it's all happening. Behind all that collapses
the shadows remain, only shadows.

¶

Dix heures vingt-cinq à l'horloge
de Bologne, le temps s'est arrêté.

Les ruines retentissent encore
sous les mots du poème
de Margherita Guidacci qui sauve
la vie des mots, – sauve-t-elle celle du passant
demeuré immobile devant l'horloge?

Les cris font des cercles de fumée
au-dessus des trains qui ne partent
plus, ne rentrent pas
en gare, ne transportent
aucun rêve, aucun désir
– rouillent sur les rails silencieux.

¶

Obscure, dénudée
parmi les ossements du siècle
la marée s'agrandit.

Tu touches l'onde froide
qui rampe jusqu'à tes lèvres.
Tu écartes les doigts, déchires
la blessure qui descend

¶

Ten twenty-five says the clock
in Bologna, time has stopped.

The ruins still echo
beneath the words of Margherita
Guidacci's poem as it saves the life
of words – does it save too the life of the passer-by
standing still in front of the clock?

The cries make smoke-rings
over the trains that no longer
go anywhere, no longer stop
at the stations, carry
no dream, no desire
– rust on their silent rails.

¶

Dark, naked
in the century's boneyard
the tide swells.

You touch the cold wave
that rises to your lips.
You spread your fingers, tear
the wound which runs down

45

au cœur de chaque faille
– répand son haleine.

Regarde ce qui fut défait
à l'horizon, regarde le cortège: l'aube
par tant de reflets s'est rompue.

¶

Tu longes le décor, poings liés
derrière le dos, la silhouette
grandit encore.

Tes regards, peu à peu
épuisent l'ombre
parmi les cils.

Un enfant s'arrête
au milieu du fracas, le corps
comme une branche, se casse

et les fleurs rebondissent
sur le mur de ta chambre.

¶

Rien. Toujours rien.
Les rapaces volent, les vipères rampent.

to the heart of every flaw
– casts its breath.

See what was unravelled
on the horizon, watch the cortège: dawn
broken by so many reflections.

¶

You follow the contours
wrists tied behind your back, still
your silhouette grows.

Little by little, your eyes
dissolve the darkness
beyond their lashes.
A child stops
amid the noise, the body
like a branch, breaks

and the flowers spring back
over your bedroom wall.

¶

Nothing. Still nothing.
The hawks fly, the vipers crawl.

L'histoire égrène de grands titres.
Tu ouvres à peine les yeux

à peine la bouche, et les mots brûlent
au bout de tes doigts, ce monde en friche
file droit sur les falaises du passé. Le fleuve
et l'oiseau percent une brèche: un rêve
remue encore parmi les ruines.

Tu effleures l'onde fragile, – sais-tu
la vie entière qu'elle porte?

¶

Et tout au bout, la cime
des rochers, le jour désossé, mis en pièces

la lourde constellation
s'arrache au poids des choses.

Écoute
le ciel, – un nuage le traverse
pousse du pied le paysage.

Tu fixes la fenêtre sans bords
que perce la route, tu imagines
la colline qu'elle explore
comme la langue, un visage.

History recites its greatest hits.
You barely open your eyes

barely open your mouth, and the words burn
your fingertips, this fallow world
slips over the cliffs of the past. The river
and the bird breach a dam: a dream
still stirring in the ruins.

You touch the fragile wave, – do you know
how much of life it holds?

¶

And at the very end, the rocks'
peak, the day in pieces, boned

the heavy constellation
tears itself from the weight of things.

Listen
the sky, – a cloud crossing it
kicks back the landscape.

You fix your eyes on the borderless window
pierced by the road
imagine the hill it explores
like a language, like a face.

¶

Le balcon vacille, on se bouscule
pour la première ligne, le dernier mot
le jour d'avant, le jour d'après.

On met la main dans la poche du vent
on en tire de maigres flocons
qui flottent comme des corps
et bientôt s'écrasent

contre les arbres pourris, l'hiver glacial
la terre sèche, les murs incendiés des bâtiments
les mâts où pendent des voiles que l'on déchire
et traînent les drapeaux décolorés
le banc où l'on passe le temps, les trottoirs
où l'on perd son visage
les rues où il se fait si tard
les compteurs désormais expirés.

¶

Si loin nous poussent les ombres
pareilles à des taches
d'encre opaque, – résidus de temps
que recueillent nos bouches.

Le voyage s'achève
et recommence

¶

The balcony sways, people
are jostling to get the first line, the last word
the day before, the day after.

We dig our hands into the wind's pocket
take out a few thin flakes
that float like bodies
and soon break

against the rotten trees, the icy winter
the dry earth, the buildings' scorched walls
the masts where the torn sails hang
and discoloured banners flap
the bench where we kill time, the pavements
where we lose ourselves
the streets where it's so late
all the meters have expired.

¶

The shadows push us so far
like spreading stains
of dark ink, – time's residues
our lips gather up.

The journey ends
and starts again

51

– vents, épaves, nos langues
claquent et balbutient –

d'aubes en crépuscules
de chair et d'os, le corps
craquelle, dans les mains
le sable ronge les pierres.

¶

Orages et noces annoncés –
le vent casse dans nos bouches, nos mots
s'éparpillent – chevilles, hanches frêles –
chaque veine bientôt s'emplit d'images
tenaces (*crèvent-elles*
tes yeux clos?).

Nous venons d'un monde irréparable, – dédales et luttes
inutiles, fragments d'os qui plongent
plongent au centre du puits où se terrent les rêves

> – et les mondes se nourrissent
> les uns les autres. Comment
> l'ignorer si longtemps?

La pente est lente
de nos âpres souvenirs, et la neige

lente entre nos doigts brûlés
> (*qui les brûle encore*).

– winds, shipwrecks, our tongues
clacking, stumbling –

dawns into dusks
of flesh and bone, the body
crazes, crackles, in our hands
the sand gnaws the stones.

¶

Storms and marriages are forecast –
the wind breaks inside our mouths, our words
scatter – ankles, frail haunches, –
each vein soon fills with insistent
images (*are they piercing
your closed eyes?*).

We come from a world beyond repair, – useless
mazes and struggles, fragments of bone plunging
plunging into the well where dreams have gone to ground

                    – and the worlds feed
                    each other. How
                    did we not see that?

The climb
of our bitter memories is slow, and the snow

slow in our burned fingers
                    (*it burns them still*).

III

SEIZING : MIRRORS
RAVIR : LES MIROIRS

¶

Le vent. – Et tu chutes
dans le paysage:
l'onde silencieuse
enserre tes pas, tes mains.

Au loin le jour brûlé
bascule. Le ciel se rompt
avec les oiseaux
venus à ta rencontre.

¶

Bouche que traversent les fleuves
– toute vie s'y broie, étrangère
au souffle et à la nuit
qui la soulèvent, vers elle-même –

pierre qu'emporte le sable.
D'aucun voyage tu ne reviens
sans que ta vie, du rivage
encore lointain, ne s'approche.

¶

De l'ombre dans la voix
tel un peu de sable

¶

The wind. – And you're falling
through the landscape:
the silent wave
closes around your steps, your hands.

Far off the burned-out day
tilts. The birds tear up
the sky as they come
to meet you.

¶

Mouth that the rivers cross
– where all life is crushed, a stranger
to the wind and the night
that lift it, towards itself –

stone carried off by the sand.
There's no journey you return from
without your life, from its
far-off bank, coming closer.

¶

Some shadow in the voice
like a little sand

s'écoule. Tu renverses
la tête: vois-tu

le temps qui s'engouffre
derrière tes mots, vois-tu
l'averse patiente?

¶

Les flèches tombent
au centre des eaux
qui vacillent aussitôt
– la plaie

sur le dos du lac
brouille le soir
qui cherchait à venir.

¶

La lutte lente
du désordre
– insaisissable
comme l'ombre

qui l'enserre –
s'étire dans le cœur.

running. You throw back
your head: do you see

time sinking
behind your words, do you see
the patient downpour?

¶

Arrows plunge
into the water
and the water trembles
– the wound

on the lake's back
obscures the night
that tried to fall.

¶

The slow struggle
of chaos
– unseizable
like the shadow

which encloses it –
stretches along the heart.

Seul le temps
nous fut donné

seule l'énigme.

¶

Nuit. – Et sur l'eau
s'agite le clair chemin.
Des visages, des corps
resurgissent. L'un

la ville l'appelle
l'Ange Haut.

¶

Tu croyais voir
du mauve, ce peu de bleu
mêlé aux miettes
que fait le jour

sur le monde.
Tu ouvres la bouche
ouvres les mains
et tout ce qui tenait encore

d'un souffle
bascule en toi.

Time was all we
were given

only mystery.

¶

Night. – And on the water
the clear path trembles.
Faces, bodies
surge back up. One of them

the city names
l'Ange Haut.

¶

You thought you saw
some mauve, a little blue
mixed with the crumbs
the day casts

over the world.
You open your mouth
open your hands
and everything that still held

by a breath
topples inside you.

¶

Terre. – Et le ciel
révèle une pierre
remplie d'azur.
Au large se débat-elle

contre l'obscur
visage du temps
se débat-elle?

¶

Ce soir, la lune
tranche le lac, creuse
un puits de silence
abrupt à l'horizon.

Le monde tressaille
– les yeux clos
tu le traverses.

¶

Est-ce ici, la nuit
sous les toits rouges
– le cœur loin devant
projeté?

¶

Earth. – And the sky
unveils a stone
full of azure.
On the open sea, is it fighting

time's
dark face
is it fighting?

¶

Tonight, the moon
slices the lake, digs
a sheer well of silence
on the horizon.

The world trembles
– eyes closed
you cross it.

¶

Is it here, the night
under the red roofs
– your heart thrown
up ahead?

Est-ce ici, la nuit
– nuée de pierres
posées sur le seuil –
qui demeure muette?

¶

Roses partout. Le corps
au milieu du jardin
jeté comme un appel.
Souffle

– et le bouquet
qu'assaillent les années
bientôt se dépoussière.

¶

Quelle ombre
défait l'aube
parmi les heures?
Quelle parole

en miettes, chaque fois
reconstruit-elle?

Is it here, the night
– stone shadows
laid on the threshold –
that stays mute?

¶

Roses everywhere. The body
at the centre of the garden
launched like a cry.
Breathe

– and the scent
worn away by the years
soon shines.

¶

What shadow
undoes the dawn
hour by hour?
What fragmented

word is it piecing back together
time after time?

¶

Le vent. – Et le lac
remue soudain, l'obscur
troupeau de vagues
s'abat contre la rive

se fond à la terre
où passent nos visages
– et se dispersent
dans la poussière.

¶

Tu suis la route
qui déchire le désert
– parmi collines
et vallées, vois:

des mondes frêles
dressent leurs tours
frissonnent à peine.

¶

Maintenant la porte
de la maison s'entrouvre:

¶

The wind. – And the lake
stirs suddenly, the dark
herd of waves
stampedes the bank

melts into the earth
where our faces pass
– scattering
into dust.

¶

You follow the road
that tears the desert
– among hills
and valleys, see:

frail worlds
raise their towers
barely trembling.

¶

Now the door
of the house is ajar:

travaux de cendre sur les murs.
Ici pénètre le souffle, – l'écho

froissé dans nos bouches –
là se tient la brèche
qui ébranle le soir.
Près du feu, ton visage

effleure la cime.

¶

Nuit. – Et l'ombre révèle
le reflet, pur miroir
des années qui dérivent
derrière tes yeux. – Pourquoi

tant de ciels
dévalent devant ta bouche?

¶

Tu disperses les jours
de lourds châteaux
parmi les ans, une voix
tranche l'ombre

mouvementée des mots
– résonne dans le foyer des mains.

the ash's work along the walls.
The breath reaches in here, – the distorted

echo in our mouths –
there is the breach
mining the night.
Near the fire, your face

brushes the tip.

¶

Night. – And the shadow discloses
the reflection, pure
mirror of the years drifting
behind your eyes. – Why

so many skies
sloping down to your mouth?

¶

You scatter the days
heavy castles
among the years, a voice
splits the words'

shifting shadow
– echoes in your hands' hearth.

¶

L'escalier, la fenêtre
par où boit le jour.
Tu vois le désordre
laissé par les chemins.

Est-ce la mer
– ou l'île –
qu'a défait ton regard?

¶

Le port. – Et l'horizon
se berce devant tes yeux
l'eau – le chaos –
rompt avec le ciel.

Tu mâches les restes
de silence que la terre
n'a pas brûlés.

¶

Le vent. La pluie. Le torrent
heurte ton corps, déverse une boue
qui creuse des tranchées
– lourde besogne

¶

The staircase, the window
the day drinks from.
You see the mess
strewn along the paths.

Is it the sea
or the island –
that your gaze dismantled?

¶

The port. – And the horizon
rocks before your eyes
the water – the chaos –
breaks with the sky.

You chew over
the scraps of silence
the earth left unburned.

¶

The wind. The rain. The flood
crashes against your body, unleashes a mud
that digs out trenches
– heavy work

sur le frêle paysage
brusquement qui s'efface.

¶

Bientôt la mer, bientôt
l'intime bouillonnement
de ta vie sur le sable
la lente empreinte du vent

les os brisés
que répand le tumulte
au milieu du monde, vois-tu
les grains s'éparpillent.

on the delicate landscape
now suddenly effaced.

¶

Soon the sea, soon
the intimate bubbling
of your life on the sand
the slow imprint of the wind

broken bones
the violence spreads
into the world, do you see
the seeds scatter.

IV

Seizing : Windows
Ravir : les fenêtres

¶

Une fenêtre. Presque le mur déjà.

Comme si l'on avait déplacé
la fenêtre, et la fenêtre seule.

Les livres se défont, les feuilles
se perdent dans l'orbite du ciel
– plus aucune couleur
et le vent manque soudain.

Qu'as-tu gardé des jardins fastes
des ombres au petit matin
qui venaient s'échouer sur tes lèvres?

À l'instant bouge le paysage. L'heure
n'est qu'un maigre abri, les arbres déploient
cornes et lames. Écoute
les années qui résonnent derrière toi
l'orage brouille tes yeux, tes mains
ne touchent plus que ce passé furieux.
Tout est rouge, bientôt sera mauve.

¶

L'arbre s'emplit
peu à peu de saisons
tapies au creux des racines.

¶

A window. Almost the wall already.

As if the window had been moved
and only the window.

The books come unbound, the leaves
are lost in the sky's orbit
– no more colours
and suddenly no wind.

What is left of the beautiful gardens
of the early morning shadows
coming to rest on your lips?

Suddenly the landscape shifts. The hour
is no more than a frail shelter, the trees unfurl
horns and blades. Listen
to the years echoing behind you
the storm blurs your vision, your hands
reach only for this furious past.
Everything is red, will soon be mauve.

¶

Little by little
the tree fills up, seasons
embedded in its roots.

Tu vois le chemin: de longs rayons
où se bousculent les personnages
de tes vies complètes. Dans ta bouche
brusquement, les mâchoires
se referment sur l'une d'elles.

¶

D'une fenêtre à une autre, le monde
remue à la surface d'un nuage
comme au fond de la mer
les livres l'emportent.

Le paysage s'embrouille
tu commences à respirer.

Tu comptes les vagues qui s'abattent
au-dessus de toi, et les histoires soudain
basculent sur la plage de silence
que découvre la dernière page.

¶

Tu ouvres la boîte où s'agite la mémoire.
Une cafetière, des gants, des bijoux et les carnets
qui alors t'accompagnaient, pêle-mêle
tu retrouves une à une tes histoires
– une foule d'images

You see the path: long rays
where the *dramatis personae* of your
unfinished lives are jostling. In your mouth
jaws suddenly close
on one of them.

¶

From one window to another, the world
stirs on the surface of a cloud
as on the seabed
books carry it away.

The landscape starts to cloud over
you start to breathe.

You count the waves that break
above you, the stories suddenly
crowding the shore of silence
opening on the final page.

¶

You open the box where memory stirs.
A cafetière, gloves, jewellery and the notebooks
you took with you everywhere back then, pell-mell
one by one, you find the stories again
– a crowd of images

assaillent chaque objet. Sais-tu
ce qui rôde dans l'autre boîte
jamais ouverte, tes histoires
jamais vécues?

¶

Tu soupèses le livre, les visages
qu'il dévore comme des ombres
absentes, sur les murs, tout
n'est que feuilles en feu
vent qui l'accable, et le mystère
demeure entier.

Les mots s'entassent, s'affolent
soudain on brûle les ombres
autour de toi. Ta vie disparaît
entre les pages qui s'ouvrent.

¶

La rumeur frissonne
tu reconnais la voix de Virginia Woolf
les tours, les îles de mots
qui renversent son corps
comme les vagues, s'échouent
contre le mur de ta chambre d'hôtel
sur Kensington, devenue chambre à soi
au cœur de Londres, les rues

fastens itself to every object. Do you know
what lurks in the other box
the one you never opened, the stories
you never lived?

¶

You weigh up the book, the faces
it eats up like absent
shadows on the walls, everywhere
leaves in flame
wind battering, the mystery
staying intact.

The words pile up, panic
suddenly they're burning
shadows around you. Your life disappears
between the open pages.

¶

The wind shakes
you recognise Virginia Woolf, her voice
the towers, the islands of words
turning her body over like waves, breaking
against the walls of your Kensington
hotel room, become now a room of one's own
in the heart of London, the streets

te mènent jusqu'à la Cathédrale
St-Paul où tu marcheras
– arpentant le Coin des Poètes –
parmi les noms usés de Hopkins
Henry James à sa gauche, et plus loin, Dylan
Thomas résonne au-dessus de T. S. Eliot.

¶

Sur les rayons, les livres convoquent
ces mondes de papier que tu caresses
du bout du doigt, de la main, – et ta vie
entière s'y enfouit.

Mers, montagnes, saisons
soufflent des histoires, et l'invisible
cède sous le poids.

À peine entrée, n'effleures-tu déjà
que le secret d'une âme?

¶

Une table basse, deux chaises
face à face, ton cœur et le mien. Tu ouvres
une fenêtre et l'on respire
les feuilles infimes, branches, bourgeons.

lead you to St Paul's
where you'll walk
– climbing Poets' Corner –
among the well-thumbed names of Hopkins
Henry James to his left, further on, Dylan
Thomas echoing above T. S. Eliot.

¶

On the shelves, the books summon up
those paper worlds your fingers stroke
your hands hold, – into which
your whole life sinks.

Seas, mountains, seasons
whisper their stories, and the invisible
gives way beneath the weight.

Barely inside, aren't you already
touching a soul's secret?

¶

A low table, two chairs
face to face, your heart and mine. You open
a window and we breathe
the tiny leaves, branches, buds.

Les papiers crépitent dans la cheminée
nos doigts se referment sur de fins pétales gris
mais les histoires tardent encore à disparaître
et le froid, et la poussière
et mon cœur avec eux.

¶

Dans la bibliothèque de Gursky
tu tournes la dernière page, c'est la fin
du livre, le monde tient donc
tout entier entre deux couvertures
se déploie puis se referme
brutalement sur des chemins
que jamais tu n'emprunteras
sinon dans le monde plein
et insoumis de tes livres.
Mais ta vie, chaque fois
ta vie s'agrandira.

¶

Seize par seize centimètres
des mots de plomb sur le papier
bouffant que déchirent les traits d'ocre
et de bleu. Les signes, tels des pas
avancent en un seul voyage.

The papers crackle in the fire
our fingers close over the fine grey petals
but the stories still won't disappear
nor the cold, nor the dust
nor my heart with them.

¶

In Gursky's library
you turn the last page, it's the end
of the book, the world that's now contained
between the covers
opens out then violently
shuts again on paths
you'll never tread
except in that rich
undefeated world of your books.
But each time, each time
your life will grow larger.

¶

Sixteen centimetres by sixteen
words of lead on soft paper
torn by lines of ochre
and blue. Signs, like steps
moving forward in a single journey.

La lumière disperse des pierres
que le temps casse dans tes mains.

¶

Goethe Rilke Rûmî Montaigne
– sous la langue roulent les eaux
l'Enfer de Dante et celui de Marina
Tsvetaïeva, chacun rend à l'autre
l'encre qu'il lèche sur la feuille jaunie.

Le gouffre, le mirage que l'œil dévoile.

Ulysse s'éveille au milieu du brouillard
Ithaque s'efface, trop loin dans l'histoire
où se faufilent tes pas. Peut-être le bruit
du passé allège-t-il l'obscur voyage?

¶

Un rideau de vent brouille la voix
du poète qui cherche à brûler le silence.
Les vagues une à une s'affaissent, déjà
délavent l'image de couverture, et la foudre
s'acharne sur les phrases qu'elle brise à mesure.

The light scatters the stones
that time breaks in your hands.

¶

Goethe Rilke Rûmi Montaigne
– the waters roll under the tongue
Dante's Hell and Tsvetaeva's
each one gives the other
the ink to lick off the yellowed page.

The abyss, the mirage the eye sees through.

Ulysses wakes in mist
Ithaca fades, too far gone in history
where your steps thread their way.
Maybe it's the sound of the past
that lightens our journey through the darkness?

¶

A curtain of wind scrambles the voice
of the poet trying to burn through the silence.
One by one the waves collapse, already
washing out the cover image, and the lightning
tears into the lines it scatters around it.

Bientôt le courant sera le chemin
le ciel boueux, l'île noyée, – quelle page
devrait-on arracher ?

¶

Tu refermes la fenêtre, refermes le monde
qui chaque fois dénoue l'histoire
– sauve l'enfant, sauve la maison de l'enfant –
comme sur les écrans minuscules
des bandes dessinées jusqu'à tes versions latines
et Raine, Barnes, Bishop
– tant que tu tiens
des mots entre les mains
le jardin où ce soir, comme tous les autres soirs
tu t'exposes au passage du vent
raconte vraiment ce qu'est la vie.

Soon the current will be the path
the muddy sky, the drowned island, – what page
must we tear out?

¶

You close the window, close the world
that each time unties your story
– save the child, save the child's house –
as from the tiny screens of comic strips
all the way to your Latin translations
and Raine, Barnes, Bishop
– so long as you hold
words in your hands
the garden where tonight, as every night
you open yourself to the wind's passage
will tell you what life really is.

V

SEIZING : FACES
RAVIR : LES VISAGES

¶

La poésie est comme un coup porté au monde par-dedans.
Valère Novarina

Soudain nos visages se couvrent de boue
s'enfoncent dans les eaux du passé.
Vers quelle rencontre allais-je
comme s'ouvre la plaie
que soupèse le temps?

Devant moi le désert
déployait des sillons de sable. Plus loin
le vent s'enroulait aux rouages
fragiles du ciel. Mon ombre
longeait cette frontière de poussière
qui ne vient de nul puits
et ne mène vers nul souffle.

Le brouillard peu à peu s'était levé.

*Tout est passager: nous avons oublié la possibilité de nous
arrêter et de regarder.*
Roberto Juarroz

¶

Poetry is like a blow struck at the world from the inside.
Valère Novarina

Suddenly our faces are covered in mud
plunge into the waters of the past.
What meeting was I going to
the way a wound opens
weighed by time?

The desert spread its furrows
of sand before me. Further on
the wind twisted around the sky's
delicate clockwork. My shadow
crept along the dust frontier
that comes from no well
and leads to no breath.

The fog little by little had lifted.

All is fleeting: we have forgotten how to stop and look.
Roberto Juarroz

93

¶

Par-dessus la colline, un nuage
rougi s'agrippe à cette heure
où se pose l'âme
– et se dissipe.
Comme en moi-même, j'entre
dans le cœur fissuré du crépuscule.

Entre mes mains, de terre et d'eau
son visage secoue des chemins de feu
– mondes frêles que ses lèvres
à peine effleurent.

Lentement ses paupières
mâchonnent mon visage
– peut-être mon âme
dans sa bouche est-elle à nouveau
en train de se faire
et de se défaire.

Émerveillée, je regarde
par la serrure du monde
j'ouvre les yeux, j'ouvre la main
comme si j'avais été invitée
à cueillir la rose de mon propre jardin.

> *En réalité c'est seulement en me voyant dans l'autre que je*
> *peux me voir, c'est seulement dans le miroir d'une autre vie*
> *semblable à la mienne que j'acquiers la certitude de ma réalité.*
> Maria Zambrano

¶

Over the hill, a reddened
cloud grips that hour
when the soul settles
– and disperses.
As into myself, I enter
the cracked heart of dusk.

Between my hands, made of earth and water
the face shakes paths of fire
– frail worlds the lips
barely touch.

Slowly the eyelids
chew my face
maybe my soul
in its mouth is making
and unmaking itself.

Dazzled, I watch
through the world's keyhole
open my eyes, open my hand
as if I had been invited
to pick the rose from my own garden.

In reality it is only by seeing myself in the other that I can
see myself, only in the mirror of another life like mine that
I can gain the certainty of my own existence.

Maria Zambrano

¶

Par tant de visages, j'entre
en mon visage.

Lente figure des ans
que nous révèlent les lunes
– lentes cavités des heures.

L'argile entre mes mains
peu à peu se liquéfiait, mon visage
se mettait à naître.

La rive déjà disparaissait
loin derrière, et loin, l'espace
bref où le rêve surgit.

J'assistais au paysage.
Je commençais à voir.

¶

Sans mesure, le souffle du Pianiste
s'enfonce dans la tempête. Les vagues

avalent la côte des souvenirs
où repose ton enfance.

¶

Through so many faces, I enter
my own face.

Slow outline of the years
revealed by so many moons
– slow cavities of hours.

Clay in my hands
slowly became liquid, my face began
to be born.

Already the bank was fading
behind us, and far away, the brief
space where dream surges up.

I was witnessing the place.
I was starting to see.

¶

Out of time, the Pianist's breathing
drowns in the storm. The waves

swallow up the coast of memories
where your childhood rests.

Dans ta bouche, les mots brûlent
ne laissent que des syllabes cassées
– chaque fois le pain, chaque fois le vin –
mais le mal s'enfonce encore.

Le jour continue
derrière la ligne frêle, l'ombre
des visages enfin s'apaise-t-elle?

¶

À coups de griffe sur la dure matière
le Menuisier creuse la surface
du monde, entame la chair
fouille les poches du temps.

La tête appuyée contre l'échafaud
il pense: me déguiser en dieu
danser dans les mains du désordre
jusqu'à la pierre, jusqu'à la boue.

¶

L'Errant, sur la route
voit la maison. Un flot de nuages
l'embue, – un monde désagrégé

In your mouth, words burn
leave only broken syllables
– each time the bread, each time the wine –
but the sickness digs in deeper.

The day goes on
behind the frail line, the shadow
of the faces appeased at last?

¶

Claw marks against hard matter
the Carpenter digs the world's
surface, opens the flesh
rifles through time's pockets.

Head against the scaffold
he thinks: disguise myself as a god
dance in the hands of chaos
down to the stone, down to the mud.

¶

The Wanderer on the road
sees the house. A flotilla of clouds
blurs its image, – a world in pieces

l'image envolée
la mélodie perdue
le mot échappé

que tu retrouves pas à pas
pour que l'aube, pour que la nuit
et la vie tiennent
à nouveau fermement.

¶

Il gratte la surface
du temps, surveille la voûte
d'où proviennent et les jours
et les mois et les ans.

1364, verrait-il
sur la facette frontale du monument
– le défilé des squelettes
les aiguilles, la corde, le sablier –
Prague 1364, verrait l'Horloger
s'il n'avait eu, au passage
l'œil crevé.

¶

Creux, terre trouée, c'est la nuit
de Pascal, ni onde ni matière

the image flown
the tune lost
the word escaped

which you retrace step by step
so that the dawn, so that the night
so that life can hold
together again.

¶

He scratches time's
surface, keeps watch over the vault
where the days
and the months and the years come from.

1364, he would see
on the monument's front facet
– the parade of skeletons
needles, rope, the hourglass –
the Clockmaker would see *Prague 1364*
had he not been blinded
in one eye.

¶

Hollow, the earth holed, it's Pascal's
mystic night, neither wave nor wavering

qui oscille, entre le temps et l'éternel
penser désunit, porte
au regard le cœur fragile.

Penser traverse une mer
de doutes, et lourdes imperfections
– n'aime que le pauvre
l'amour, le véritable.

¶

Tout le jour le Puisatier creuse un cercle
vers le fond de la terre
arrache la rose, aspire l'humus
pour que l'eau, pour que l'écume
comblent le vide.

Il cherche: le proche et le lointain
le trompe-l'œil, l'envers
le modèle, le lent travail
des pierres humectées par le temps.

Il trouve:
la profondeur du granit
l'orbite du monde, furieux
qui brise ses filets
et avale son soleil.

matter, between time and eternity
thought unbinding, carrying
the fragile heart into view.

Thinking crosses a sea
of doubts and heavy flaws
– loves only the poor one
love, the true one.

¶

All day long the Well-sinker digs a circle
down to the earth's core
tears up the rose, clears the soil
so that the water, so that the spume
can fill the void.

He searches: the near and the far
the *trompe-l'œil*, the inside-out
the model, the slow work
of stones slaked by time.

He finds:
granite's depth
the world's furious orbit
bursting its nets
swallowing its sun.

¶

Matière, mouvement du paysage.
On touche à l'une, sans ressentir l'autre.
Au milieu du tableau, l'histoire
déchire le paysage.

Land art
Lanyon
Lascaux caves
Long

Polke
Post Impressionism
Postmodernism
Poussin

Raphael
Realism
Renaissance
*Richter**

¶

Autour du Marcheur, la lumière
arpente l'horizon. Les pierres s'amoncellent

* Emma Kay, *The Story of Art*, Tate Modern.

¶

Matter, landscape's movement.
You touch one, can't feel the other.
In the centre of the frame, history
tears the canvas.

Land art
Lanyon
Lascaux caves
Long

Polke
Post Impressionism
Postmodernism
Poussin

Raphael
Realism
Renaissance
Richter*

¶

Around the Walker, the light climbs the horizon.
The stones heap up

* Emma Kay, *The Story of Art*, Tate Modern.

le long des chemins, – il reconnaît
les bâtiments, la ville haute
et la plaine qu'érodaient jadis
les lourds sabots des chevaux.

Il demande: par où
le lieu qui n'est aucun lieu
mais qui les porte tous.

¶

Le bois
les cordes
les clés
de métal
– la forme sinueuse
de l'instrument posé entre ses jambes
la Harpiste sème des sons, secoue la tête:

ainsi le corps, croit-elle
embrasse les notes, ainsi l'âme s'allonge
et respire sur les portées, compte le temps
puis son visage pâlit
ses mains blanches, sa peau fine
plus fine encore.

along the paths, – he recognises
the buildings, the high town
and the plain that was once eroded
by the horses' heavy hooves.

He asks: which
is the place that is not a place
but that holds them all.

¶

Wood
ropes
metal
keys
– the sinuous contours
of the instrument between her legs
the Harpist sows sounds, shakes her head:

thus does the body embrace the notes
she thinks, thus the soul stretches
and breathes along the staves, beats time
then her face pales
her white hands, her fine skin
finer still.

¶

Hypatie, par le nombre ou
la figure, pousse la porte
et du pied ses limites.

À la loi des hommes prisonniers de leur loi
soumise et rebelle, bientôt brûlée
sans foi aura-t-elle adoré d'autres dieux
et sous l'assaut des flammes

cet aveu: me pencher
comme un arbre cloué à la terre.

¶

Sous le ciel calciné
le Bâtisseur s'affaire dans le noir
tire les ligaments invisibles

cherche l'arbre
cherche la falaise.

Il dit: tant de poutres
soutiennent notre vide
comme s'étirent des racines
jusqu'à effleurer l'os.

Sans l'affaiblir, la pierre secoue l'obscurité
l'eau atone, la terre gisant au milieu.

¶

Hypatia, with numbers or
with figures, pushes open
the door, pushes back her limits.

To the law of men prisoners of their law
she is subject and in revolt, soon burned
faithless did she worship other gods
and beneath the flames' assault

this confession: I lean
like a tree pinned to the ground.

¶

Under the calcinated sky
the Builder is busy in the darkness
pulling together the invisible ligaments

searching for the tree
searching for the cliff.

He says: so many beams
are holding up our void
as the roots spread so far
they touch the bone.

Without weakening it, the stone shakes the darkness
the toneless water, the dying earth at the centre.

Et le maigre abri nous invente
maisons de flammes et châteaux de sable.

¶

J'ai été, en d'autres temps, poète
– dit le Chevalier, du haut de la tour
qui enfile son armure, affûte ses lances
prépare l'épée
qui dès l'aube tranchera le silence.

Il touche: de minuscules puits dans le ciel
qui se disputent l'obscurité.

Une forêt, un vent, à peine les traces
de son histoire. Tout suffit.

Au bas du poème, des chiens
cernent une proie, patiemment
attendent la levée du jour.

¶

La lumière pénètre douce, c'est le matin
dans la chambre de Vermeer
le Géographe déroule ses cartes, au hasard
choisit celle où les continents se bousculent
et poussent les uns sur les autres, sur le coin droit
s'entrelacent des formes inconnues, innommées.

And for us the frail shelter invents
houses of fire and castles of sounds.

¶

In other times I was a poet
– said the Horseman, from the top of the tower
putting on his armour, sharpening his lances
readying the sword
which at dawn will cut through the silence.

He touches: tiny wells in the sky
fighting over the darkness.

A forest, a wind, barely even traces
of his story. It is all enough.

At the bottom of the poem, dogs
encircle their prey, patiently
waiting for daybreak.

¶

The light penetrates softly, it's morning
in Vermeer's bedroom
the Geographer unfolds his maps, randomly
chooses the one where the continents jostle
and press each other, on the right corner
unknown shapes interlaced, unnamed.

Il regarde: le Navigateur ouvre son compas
fixe des points minuscules
délimite les jours, les mois, les ans
au-delà des naufrages, trace des routes
pour d'autres matins.

Nous sommes seuls, pense-t-il.
Le corps, l'âme. Chaque vie
disperse sa lumière
dans la chambre du temps.

¶

Passé les dunes, la pente abrupte
mène vers la mer. La perspective se modifie
légèrement, les nuages et les galets
se fondent, le vent s'éparpille sur la peau

et si l'on porte à l'oreille un coquillage
on entend murmurer chaque souvenir
laissé là, enfoui sous les marées.

Alors le Derviche, avec l'écume, avec le sable
pénètre la mesure
– l'univers, le rien –
souffle comme il danse:
secoue les draps de l'âme.

He watches: the Navigator opens his compass
fixes tiny points
parcels out the days, months, years
beyond the shipwrecks, traces routes
for other mornings.

We are alone, he thinks.
The body, the soul. Each life
scatters its light
across time's room.

¶

Beyond the dunes, the sheer slope
leads down to the sea. The view changes
a little, the clouds and the shingle
melt into each other, the wind plays on the skin

and if you hold a shell to your ear
you'll hear each memory
left buried there beneath the tides.

Then the Dervish, in time with the foam, with the sand
enters the rhythm
– the universe, the void –
breathes as he dances:
shakes the soul's sheets.

¶

Le monde dévore nos paupières
au-delà des rêves, de la rose
que mâche la nuit, nous vivons
comme des feuilles enroulées
autour de l'horizon, nous flottons
et pour guérir de nous-mêmes

– quand éclatent les fissures
que se perdent les pierres
jetées parmi les lambeaux des siècles –

nous glissons avec les continents
cherchons l'eau, cherchons le rivage
et un jour l'image se retourne
le Gardien des Lieux, à nouveau
se penche sur nous.

¶

Le chiffre trois, les yeux
du Lieur, il existerait
un monde en mesure
d'accomplir les vies innombrables

les occasions
la multitude
la diversité

¶

The world devours our eyelids
beyond our dreams, beyond the rose
eaten by the night, we live
like leaves curling
around the horizon, we float
and to cure us of ourselves

– when the cracks burst open
the stones sink
thrown to the tatters of centuries –

we drift with the continents
seeking the water, seeking the bank
and one day the image is inverted
the Keeper of the Place, once again
leans over us.

¶

The number three, the eyes
of the Weaver, there may be
a world capable
of fulfilling the innumerable lives

chances
multitude
diversity

le sens
l'effet
l'art

de la matière
– accouplées, unies, légères.

meaning
effect
art

 of matter
– entwined, united, weightless.

Hélène Dorion was born in 1958 in Quebec City, and now lives in Montreal. She studied philosophy at Laval University (Quebec), and published her first collection of poems, *L'Intervalle prolongé*, in 1983. Since then her prolific *œuvre* – poetry, fiction, essays, and livres d'artistes – has constituted one of modern Quebecois literature's major achievements. She is the winner of the Governor General's Award for Poetry, the Prix Mallarmé, the Prix Wallonie-Bruxelles, the Prix Alain-Grandbois, and numerous other Canadian and international prizes. When *Ravir: les lieux* appeared in 2005, Dorion became the first Canadian to receive the Prix Mallarmé, while her 2008 volume, *Le Hublot des heures*, won the Prix Charles-Vildrac – another first for a Quebecois writer. In 2011, Dorion won the European Prix Léopold-Senghor. A selection of her poetry in English appeared in 2004 with the title *No End to the World: Selected Poems*, translated by Daniel Sloate and published by Guernica Editions.

www.helenedorion.com

Patrick McGuinness was born in Tunisia in 1968 and is now Professor of French and Comparative Literature at the University of Oxford, where he is a Fellow of St Anne's College. He is the author of two collections of poems, *The Canals of Mars* and *Jilted City* (both published by Carcanet), a novel, *The Last Hundred Days* (long-listed for the Booker Prize, short-listed for the Costa First Novel Award, and winner of the Wales Book of the Year 2012), and several academic books about French literature and modern poetry. In 2009 he was made Chevalier des Palmes académiques for services to French culture, and in 2011 Chevalier des Arts et des Lettres.
He lives in Caernarfon, Wales.

www.patrickmcguinness.org.uk

Uzia Ograbek (cover artist) is an artist and illustrator, born Cracow in 1974. Resident in Venice since 1999, she has exhibited in numerous solo and group shows in Poland, Italy, Germany, Slovenia and China.

www.uziaograbek.eu